Architectural Styles

CARSON DUNLOP & ASSOCIATES

Dearborn™
Real Estate Education

This publication is designed to provide accurate and authoritative information in regard to the subject matter covered. It is sold the understanding that the publisher is not engaged in rendering legal, accounting, or other professional service. If legal or other expert assistance is required, the services of a competent professional person should be sought.

Presi. Roy Lipner
Publishei Director of Distance Learning: Evan M. Butterfield
Senior Develo, nt Editor: Laurie McGuire
Content Consultant: Alan Carson
Production Coordinator: Daniel Frey
Creative Director: Lucy Jenkins
Graphic Design: Neglia Design Inc.

► TABLE OF CONTENTS

ACKNOWLEDGMENTS

Thanks to Kevin O'Malley for his inspiration, advice and guidance. Thanks also to James Dobney for his invaluable input and encouragement. Special thanks are extended to Dan Friedman for his numerous and significant contributions.

We are grateful for the contributions of: Duncan Hannay, Richard Weldon, Peter Yeates, Tony Wong, Graham Clarke, Ian Cunliffe, Joe Seymour, Charles Gravely, Graham Lobban, Dave Frost, Gerard Gransaull, Jim Stroud, Diana DeSantis, David Ballantyne, Shawn Carr and Steve Liew.

Special thanks are also extended to Susan Bonham, Dearbhla Lynch, Lucia Cardoso-Tavares, Jill Brownlee, Ida Cristello and Rita Minicucci-Colavecchia who have brought everything together. Thanks also to Jim Lingerfelt for his invaluable editing assistance.

► 1.0 OBJECTIVES

At the end of this book, you should be able to identify the common architectural styles and features used in your area.

► 2.0 INTRODUCTION

2.1 INTRODUCTION TO ARCHITECTURAL STYLES

In this section, we are going to discuss some of the common architectural styles of homes and some architectural features that you should be able to recognize.

Credit

This section is substantially based on a book entitled *A Field Guide to American Houses* by **Virginia and Lee McAlester** published by **Alfred A. Knopf, Inc**. You may want to get a copy of this very good book for your library.

*Just
Scratching
The Surface*

Our discussion will be superficial. We're trying to give a general practitioner's knowledge, not to turn you into a specialist. We apologize in advance for omitting your favorite type of house or not going into enough detail on the architectural elements you are most interested in.

*Focus On
The Exterior*

While architectural styles relate to the interior as well as the exterior of the building, we're going to focus on the exterior. This is a common approach, although it's not always reliable.

Architectural Styles
M O D U L E

STUDY SESSION 1

1. This section deals with some of the common building shapes and their respective roofing styles that help form the shape of a building.

2. At the end of this Study Session, you should be able to –

- distinguish detached, semi-detached, and attached house types.
- explain in one sentence how floor plans can be used to distinguish between different styles of houses.
- list at least five types of sloped roofs.
- explain in one sentence the functions of roof overhangs.
- describe in two sentences how chimneys and dormers can be used to enhance the architectural style of a home.
- list at least six common dormer shapes.

3. Quick Quiz 1 is included at the end. The answers can be written in your book.

Key Words:

- *Row house*
- *Duplex*
- *Linear plan*
- *Massed*
- *Cape Cod*
- *Saltbox*
- *Four-square*
- *Butterfly roof*
- *Gambrel*
- *Dutch Colonial*
- *Mansard*
- *Bell-cast eave*
- *Pinnacle*
- *Cupola*
- *Turret*
- *Cresting*
- *Widow's walk*
- *Vergeboard*
- *Dormers — hip, gable, shed, flat, eyebrow, segmental, arched, inset*

► 3.0 BUILDING SHAPES & DETAILS

Most single-family homes are substantially rectangular. They can be one-story, one-and-a-half-story, two-story, two-and-a-half-story or three-story. Split-level houses have adjacent sections a half story above or below each other. These may be sidesplit or backsplit.

Houses can be longer in one direction than the other. Houses can also be boxes, with all four walls being equal length. Many houses are a combination of rectangles, with wings or T's off a main box. While curved walls are less common, you will find some. Walls that intersect each other at something other than a right angle are also less common, but you will find them.

3.1 DETACHED, SEMIDETACHED AND ATTACHED

In rural areas, houses are almost always **detached.** In urban settings, houses may be detached or they may share one wall with their neighboring house. These houses are called **semidetached** in many areas. Where more than two houses are attached, they are often called **row houses** or, in some areas, **townhomes.** A detached building with a separate residence on the main floor and a different home on the second floor is called a **duplex.** In some areas, duplexes may also mean two dwelling units side by side in a single building.

3.2 FLOOR PLANS

Floor plans of houses vary widely and may be complex. However, with very few exceptions, they are made up of a number of simple elements. We've talked about houses being one, one-and-a-half, two, two-and-a-half or three stories in height. We can also look at the depth of the house. A **linear plan** house, for example, is essentially one room deep. A **massed house** is typically two rooms deep.

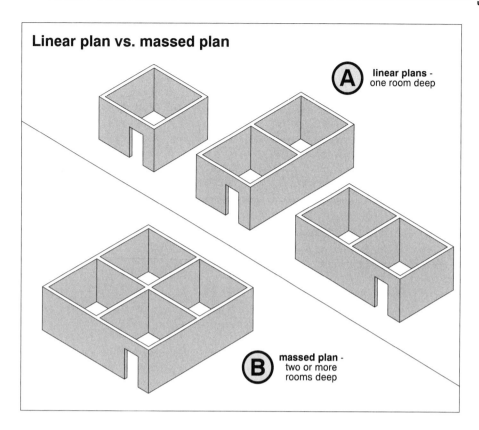

Linear plan vs. massed plan

(A) linear plans - one room deep

(B) massed plan - two or more rooms deep

Transitional-style houses, like **Cape Cods** and **saltboxes**, are typically one-and-a-half rooms deep. Houses that are square are typically two rooms deep and two rooms wide. These are often called **four-square** homes. Adding units to form an L, T, U or H, makes the plan **compound**.

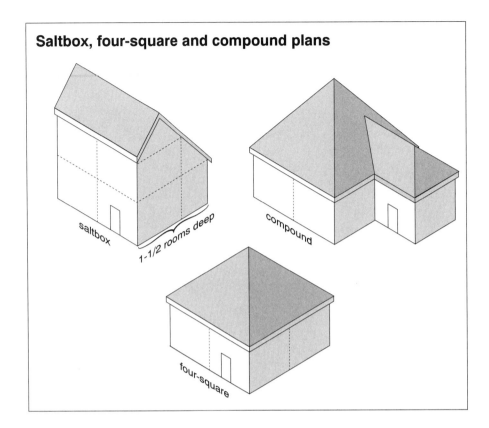

Saltbox, four-square and compound plans

saltbox

1-1/2 rooms deep

compound

four-square

Cars Affect
Floor Plans

Floor plans have changed in the last century as automobiles have become part of our life. Part of the building envelope has been given over to garages, and floor plans have changed as a result. The garage may accommodate one or two cars and may be completely within the rectangle of the house, completely external, or partly within the house rectangle.

3.3 ROOF SHAPES

The shape of a building is, in part, determined by the shape of the roof.

The simplest roof is a **flat roof**. Flat roofs may overhang the building walls or building walls may extend slightly above the roofline, forming parapets. In the latter case, there is no overhang.

Flat roofs

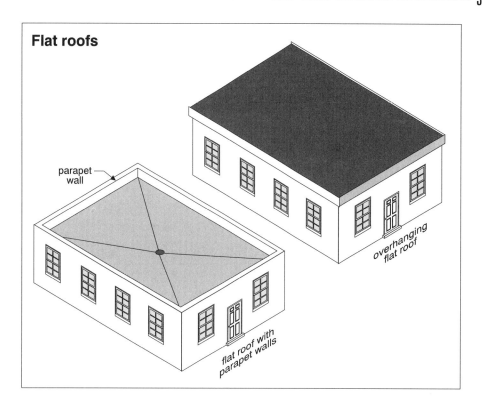

parapet wall

flat roof with parapet walls

overhanging flat roof

Sloped roofs can be many shapes:

- The simplest sloped roof is probably the **shed roof.**
- The next simplest is the **gable roof**. Gable roofs may be symmetric or asymmetric, as in the saltbox-shaped home.
- The **butterfly roof** is as simple as a gable roof, but it is not a natural shedding roof. In areas of high rainfall or snow accumulation, butterfly roofs are not common for obvious reasons.
- **Hip roofs** are another common roof shape. Hip roofs can have a ridge or come to a central point. Hip roofs that come to a single point are sometimes called **four square hip roofs**.
- **Gambrel roofs**, or **Dutch Colonial** roofs as they are sometimes called, are gable roofs with two slopes. The lower slope is steeper and the upper slope is lower.
- A **mansard** roof typically slopes on all four sides and each side has a double slope. The lower slope is very steep and may approach a wall. The upper part is typically a very low-slope roof.

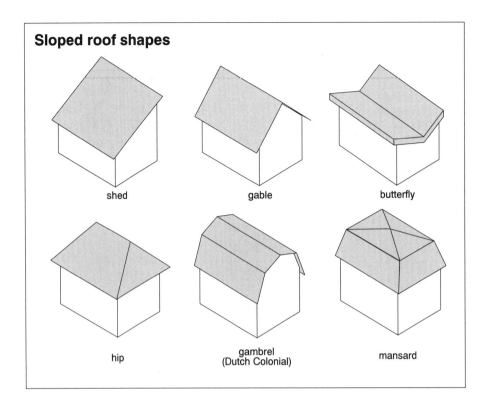

Sloped roof shapes

shed   gable   butterfly

hip   gambrel (Dutch Colonial)   mansard

Roof Plane   The plane of the roof is usually uniform. Some roofs, however have a sweep over their entire slope, or may have a flare on the lower part of the roof. This is sometimes called a **bell-cast eave**.

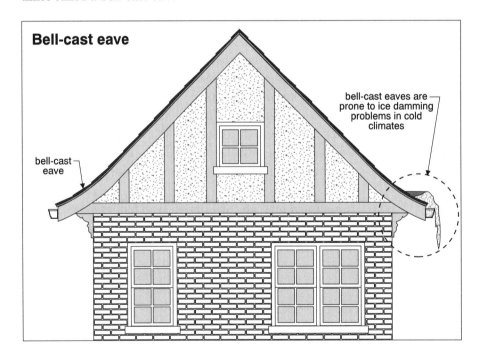

Bell-cast eave

bell-cast eaves are prone to ice damming problems in cold climates

bell-cast eave

Slope Of The Roof   The slope of the roof impacts on the shape of the building and helps to establish the style of the home. Houses with flat or low-sloped roofs have the walls as the focal point. Houses with very steep roofs often use the roof as the focal point of the house.

Roof Details   Roofs may have **pinnacles**, **cupolas** or **turrets**. Roofs may have **cresting** along the ridge or, if there is a flat roof, there may be decorative iron railings around the perimeter, often called a **widow's walk**.

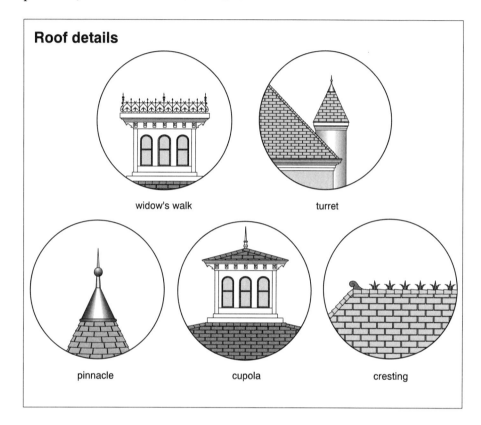

Roof details

widow's walk

turret

pinnacle

cupola

cresting

Gable Details   The edge of the roofing that sticks out along a gable is called the **verge.** Roof gables may have decorative treatments such as intricately carved **vergeboards, barge- board** or **gingerbread**, trusses in the gables, or beams projecting from the gables.

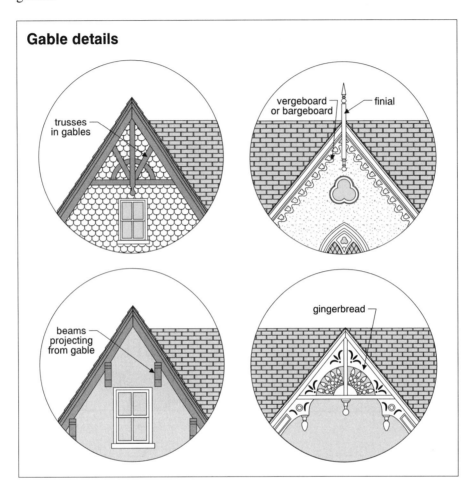

Gable details

Roof
Overhangs

The amount of overhang on a roof may strongly influence the architectural style of the house. Some roofs have no overhang, others have a modest overhang, and still others have a very pronounced roof overhang. There is a functional issue here since generous roof overhangs generally keep walls drier. As you might imagine, generous roof overhangs tend to be more popular in wet and northern climates. There are, of course, exceptions to this.

Large overhangs also help to shield windows from direct sunlight, keeping the home cooler in hot weather.

Porch Roofs   Roof overhangs are sometimes exaggerated to form roofs for porches.

Secondary
Roofs

Some homes rely on secondary roofs for much of their visual appeal. This includes roofs on dormers, bay windows and porticos, for example.

3.4 CHIMNEYS AND DORMERS

Chimneys

Chimneys and dormers can form architectural focal points of a home as well. They may be located around the perimeter of the building or on the interior. Chimneys can be small or very large. Multiple chimneys are often arranged in a symmetrical pattern (for example, at either end of the ridge on a gable house). Chimneys can be various shapes and are often a different material than the exterior wall surfaces. Decorative pots on chimney tops can be part of the visual appeal of a home.

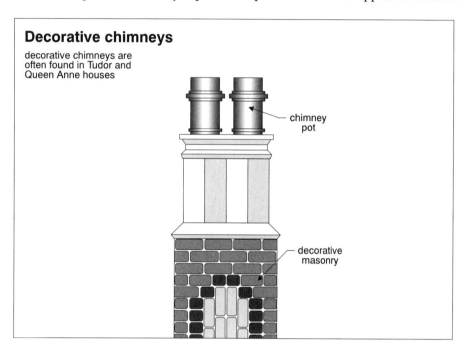

Decorative chimneys

decorative chimneys are often found in Tudor and Queen Anne houses

chimney pot

decorative masonry

Dormers   Dormers can be various shapes and sizes. They may be decorative or they may define living space. There may be one dormer or several. Common dormer shapes include **gable, shed, hip, flat, eyebrow, segmental** (shallow slope), **arched** (steep slope) and **inset**. Dormers often, but not always, include windows.

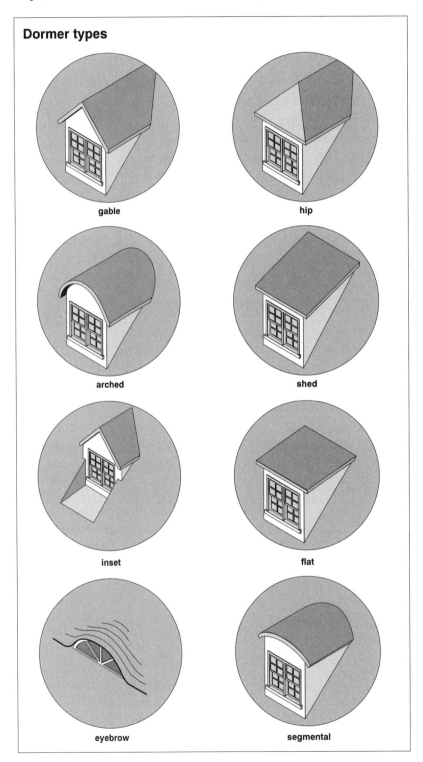

Dormer types

gable   hip

arched   shed

inset   flat

eyebrow   segmental

Architectural Styles
M O D U L E

QUICK QUIZ 1

☑ INSTRUCTIONS

• Write your answers in the spaces provided.

• Check your answers against ours at the back of the book after the Final Exercise.

• If you have trouble with the Quiz, reread the Study Session and try the Quiz again.

1. Houses are basically _____ in shape.

2. List the three terms used to describe how a house connects or relates to its neighbors.

   _____

   _____

   _____

3. Are semidetached homes more common in rural or urban environments?

   _____

4. What is the difference between a linear plan house and a massed house?

   _____

§ 1

5. Why are butterfly pitched roofs not desirable in northern climates?

_____

6. A typical barn would have what style of pitched roof?

_____

7. List six types of sloped roofs.

_____

_____

_____

_____

_____

_____

8. A gambrel roof is sometimes called _____ .

9. How does roof type affect the focal point of the house?

_____

_____

_____

10. Three types of pointed roof structures are –

_____

_____

_____

11. What elements identify a widow's walk?

_____

_____

12. What is vergeboard?

_____

13. What are three advantages of large overhangs on a house?

_____

_____

_____

14. How can chimneys and dormers be used to enhance the visual appeal of a home?

_____

15. List eight common dormer shapes.

_____

_____

_____

_____

_____

_____

_____

_____

Key Words:

- *Row house*
- *Duplex*
- *Linear plan*
- *Massed*
- *Cape Cod*
- *Saltbox*
- *Four-square*
- *Butterfly roof*
- *Gambrel*
- *Dutch Colonial*
- *Mansard*
- *Bell-cast eave*
- *Pinnacle*
- *Cupola*
- *Turret*
- *Cresting*
- *Widow's walk*
- *Vergeboard*
- *Dormers — hip, gable, shed, flat, eyebrow, segmental, arched, inset*

Architectural Styles
M O D U L E

STUDY SESSION 2

1. This section deals with building details such as window types, window shapes, doors and columns.

2. At the end of this Study Session, you should be able to –

    • list some common details that enhance or define architectural styles.
    • describe in one sentence how siding treatments can be used to distinguish between different styles of homes.
    • define various window types and describe in one sentence each how they operate.
    • identify various shapes of windows and their associated architectural styles.
    • list ten types and features of doors.
    • list four column types.

3. Quick Quiz 2 is included at the end. The answers can be written in your book.

Key Words:
- *Cornice*
- *Dentil*
- *Entablature*
- *Quoining*
- *Tudor*
- *Nogging*
- *Double-hung*
- *Single-hung*
- *Casement*
- *Sashless*
- *Awning*
- *Hopper*
- *Jalousie*
- *Muntin*
- *Gothic*
- *Palladian*
- *Fanlight*
- *Curved top*
- *Pediment*
- *Bay*
- *Oriel*
- *Bow*
- *Transom*
- *Pilaster*
- *Capital*

3.5 BUILDING DETAILS

Building details often define architectural styles, or at least architectural elements in a home. These details can include –

- the roof, chimney and dormers, as we've already discussed
- the materials used for roofing or wall cladding
- porches and their roofs, railings, and columns
- windows and doors

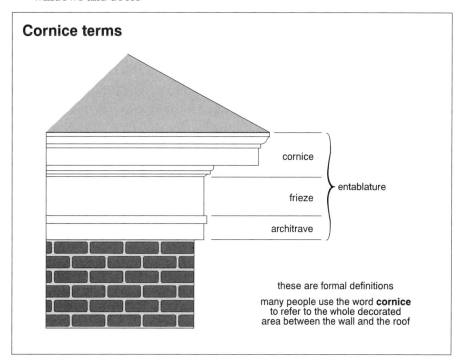

Cornice terms

cornice

frieze

architrave

entablature

these are formal definitions

many people use the word **cornice** to refer to the whole decorated area between the wall and the roof

- Decorative trim around the perimeter of the home at the top of the wall just below the roof. This area is the **cornice**, which may be decorated with trim. If this trim is fancy, it is often called an **entablature**, and has three main components: the **cornice, frieze and architrave**. The cornice may have **dentils**, a series of small rectangular closely-spaced blocks projecting down like teeth. Another decorative detail around the eaves is a **bracket** system.

Brackets versus dentils

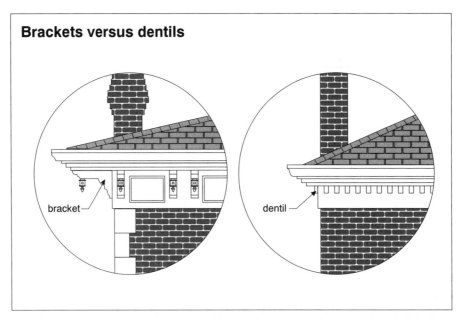

bracket

dentil

- Eaves may have closed soffits and a fascia, or the rafters may be visible from below, extending out beyond the walls.

3.6 WALL SYSTEMS

Shingles And Half-timbering

In many cases, the siding treatment itself helps define the architectural style of the home. This is true of shingle-style homes and Tudor-style homes, for example. **Shingle-style** homes have wood shingle siding. **Tudor-style** homes have **half-timbered** effects, which in most cases are decorative wood members (rather than actual structural timbers) with the spaces between filled with masonry or stucco. Brick **nogging** is another treatment that is typical of Tudor homes. Nogging refers to the filling of brick or masonry between wood posts or studs.

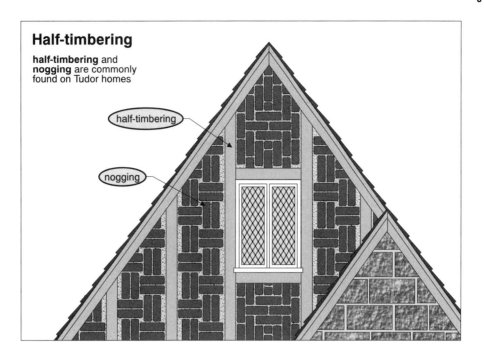

Half-timbering

half-timbering and **nogging** are commonly found on Tudor homes

half-timbering

nogging

Stucco And Adobe   Spanish-style houses are often stucco or adobe. In traditional adobe construction, the exterior walls are built of blocks made of soil mixed with straw. These wall systems help define the style.

Quoining   **Quoining** is a detail at the corners of walls, usually extending the full height of the walls. The wall corners have rectangular blocks of a different color and/or texture than the rest of the wall. Quoining may project from the face of the walls on both sides of the corner.

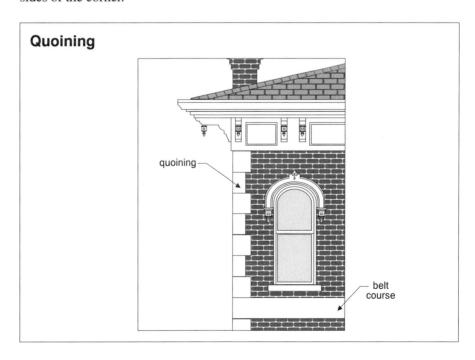

Quoining

quoining

belt course

3.7 WINDOWS

Let's define some window types by their operating methods and also discuss some window styles, based on their shape.

Operating method

Fixed Windows   **Fixed** windows are sometimes called **picture** windows. These do not open.
Double-hung   **Double-hung** windows have two operable sashes that move vertically. Many older
And Single-   homes have double-hung windows. Modern homes typically have **single-hung**
hung Windows   windows that look like double-hung windows. Very often, only the bottom part of
the window is operable.

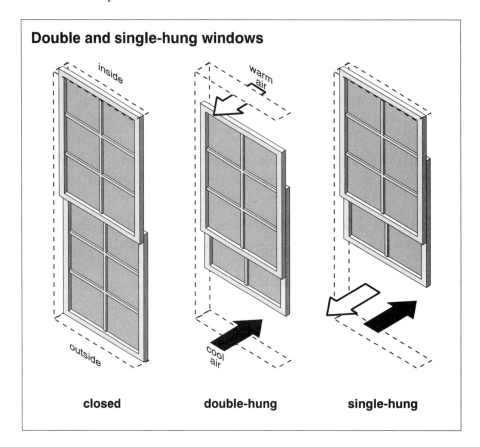

Double and single-hung windows

closed   double-hung   single-hung

Casement Windows

Casement windows are popular. They may be hinged at one side or they may pivot so that both sides of the window are accessible for cleaning from the inside. These windows may swing in or out. Most modern casement windows are crank operated. Most older casement windows are not. They will usually have some kind of stop mechanism to hold the window at the desired position.

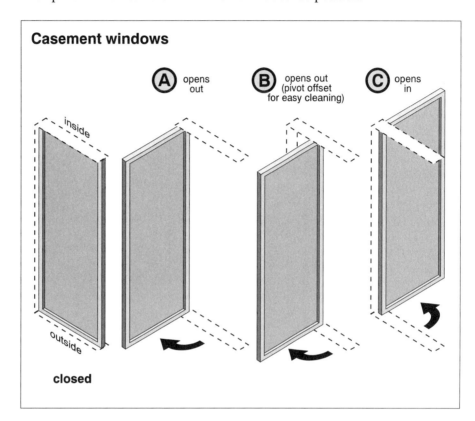

Casement windows

Ⓐ opens out Ⓑ opens out (pivot offset for easy cleaning) Ⓒ opens in

inside

outside

closed

Sliders   **Sliders** are windows that move horizontally. The entire window may be sliders, although small sliders are often located below a fixed window. Sliders often have a fixed sash and a sliding sash. These are similar to sliding patio doors. Some inexpensive sliders are **sashless**, which means the glass pane has no wood, vinyl or metal around it. The glass itself slides in a track. These are low quality windows.

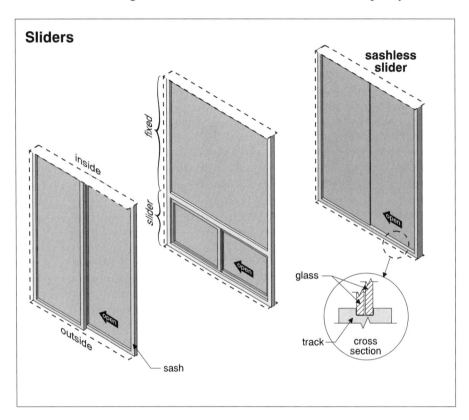

Awning Windows   **Awning** windows are hinged at their top and swing out (most often) or in. They are often crank operated.

Hopper Windows   **Hopper** windows are hinged at the bottom and typically swing in to the living space, rather than out.

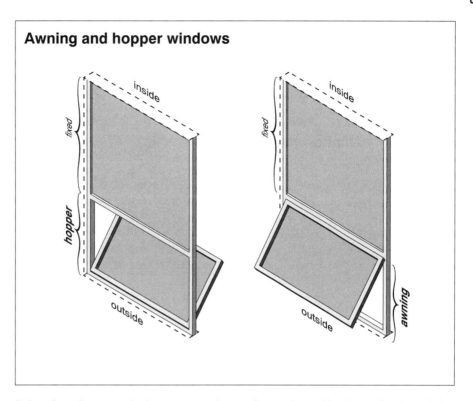

Awning and hopper windows

Jalousie Or Louver Windows

Jalousie or **louver** windows are made up of a number of horizontal strips of glass that overlap each other in a shingle pattern when closed. These windows operate a little like Venetian blinds. They are not generally very weather-tight (poor in northern climates), but are good for providing ventilation.

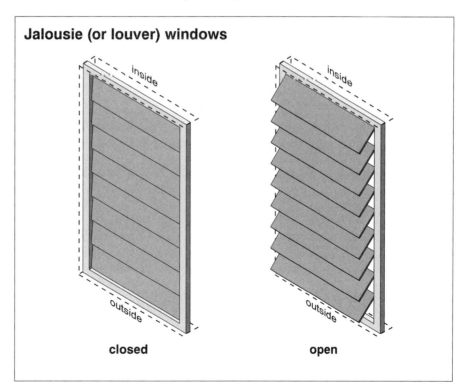

Jalousie (or louver) windows

closed   **open**

Glazing

Windows can be single-, double- or triple-pane without affecting the architectural style. Windows may have a single pane of glass in each sash or the panes may be broken by muntins. Functional muntins are typically wood or lead, although other materials can be used. The muntins in windows often help define the architectural style of the home.

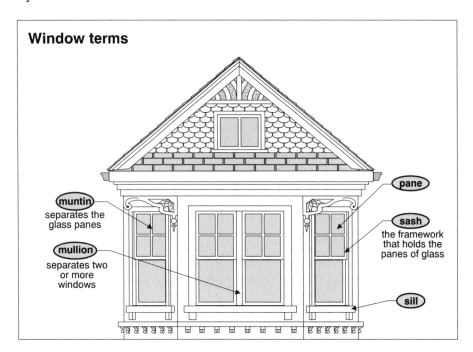

Window terms

pane

muntin
separates the
glass panes

mullion
separates two
or more
windows

sash
the framework
that holds the
panes of glass

sill

Fake Muntins

Many modern windows do not have true muntins that separate the glass into various panes. The muntins may be decorative only, mounted either on the interior face of a single pane of glass, or installed between two panes of a double glazed window assembly. The muntins that are purely decorative may be wood, plastic, metal or even a tape applied directly to the glass.

Window Shapes There are some window shapes that are characteristic of certain architectural styles.

1. **Gothic windows**, copied from European churches, have an arch that rises to a point.
2. **Palladian windows** are typically a set of three windows with the center window having a round top and the windows on either side being lower, and often narrower.
3. **Fanlight windows** are typically half circles with radial muntins and often intricate detailing.
4. **Curved-top windows** are often associated with Italianate style. They can be a half circle, or an ellipse, for example. They often have bold detailing around the windows to draw the eye to these architectural features.
5. **Lintels** and **sills** may be decorative, or there may be distinctive **crowns** or other trim around the windows to further draw attention to the window.
6. Window crowns include **hoods** and **pediments**, for example.

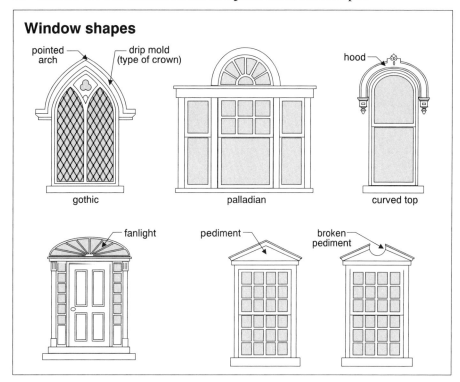

Window shapes

7. **Bay windows** project from the wall surface and extend down to the ground
8. **Oriel windows** project from the building but do not extend down to the ground.
9. **Bow windows** project from the building in a curved plane. They usually extend down to the ground.

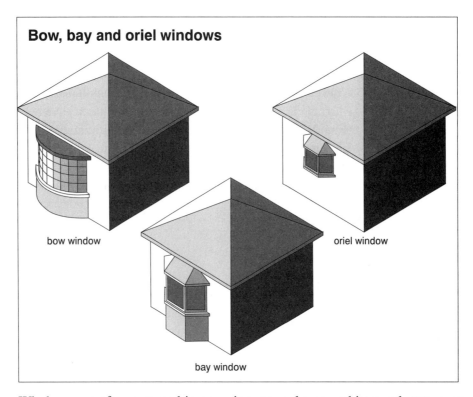

Bow, bay and oriel windows

bow window

oriel window

bay window

Groups And Shutters   Windows are often arranged in groupings to make an architectural statement. Windows may have operable or decorative shutters.

3.8 DOORS

Doors can also make an architectural statement. Doors may be single or arranged in pairs (sometimes called French doors). They can be solid or have glass. They can be simple slabs or intricately carved. They can be paneled. The top may be flat or curved.

Lights

Doors may have fanlights or **transom lights** above. They may have **sidelights** on one or both sides that may be full height or partial height. Doors may be flanked by pilasters and crowned by pediments. There may be decorative siding treatments around the door. Doors may have shutters on either side.

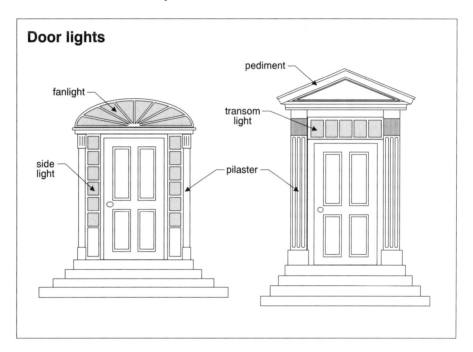

Door lights

3.9 COLUMNS

Columns can make a strong architectural statement. They may be one or two stories tall. Columns can be single or arranged in groups of two or three. They may be free standing and functional, or be simply decorative and, in some cases, built into walls. In these cases, they are really **pilasters** that are simply projections from the wall of the house. Columns can be round, square or rectangular, straight or tapered. Column styles are often defined by their **capitals**. Capitals are the tops of columns. Classic styles include **Doric, Ionic, Tuscan** and **Corinthian**.

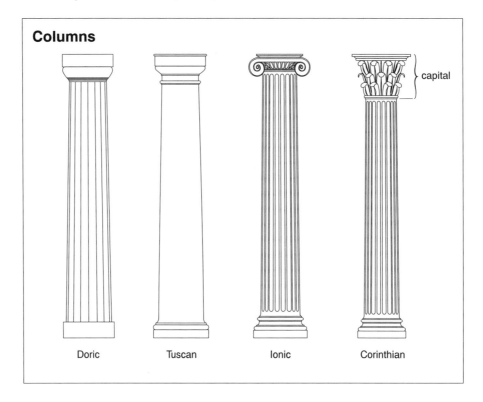

Columns

Doric   Tuscan   Ionic   Corinthian

capital

Architectural Styles
M O D U L E

QUICK QUIZ 2

☑ INSTRUCTIONS

• Write your answers in the spaces provided.

• Check your answers against ours at the back of the book after the Final Exercise.

• If you have trouble with the Quiz, reread the Study Session and try the Quiz again.

1. What is the term for fancy decorative trim at the eave area of a house?

   _____

2. What does a dentil look like and where would it be found?

   _____

   _____

3. What is quoining?

   _____

4. How can the siding treatment be used to distinguish between a Tudor-style home and a shingle-style home?

   _____

5. List six different types of windows.

    _____

    _____

    _____

    _____

    _____

    _____

6. What is a sashless slider?

    _____

7. How does a hopper window differ from an awning window?

    _____

8. Are jalousie or louver windows more desirable in warm or cool climates?

    _____

9. What is the function of a muntin?

    _____

10. Draw a small picture of the following window types:

    i) Gothic   ii) Palladian

    iii) Fanlight   iv) Curved top

11. Where would you find a hood or pediment?

_____

12. How do bay and bow windows differ from oriel windows?

_____

13. A transom light is found beside a door.
   True ☐   False ☐

14. How does a pilaster differ from a column?

_____

_____

15. List four classic column styles.

_____

_____

_____

_____

If you had no trouble with the Quiz, you are ready for Study Session 3.

Key Words:

- **Cornice**
- **Dentil**
- **Entablature**
- **Quoining**
- **Tudor**
- **Nogging**
- **Double-hung**
- **Single-hung**
- **Casement**
- **Sashless**
- **Awning**
- **Hopper**
- **Jalousie**
- **Palladian**
- **Fanlight**
- **Curved top**
- **Pediment**
- **Bay**
- **Oriel**
- **Bow**
- **Transom**
- **Pilaster**
- **Capital**
- **Gothic**
- **Muntin**

Architectural Styles
M O D U L E

STUDY SESSION 3

1. This section deals with both common and specific house styles and their defining features.

2. At the end of this Study Session, you should be able to –

- list five common house styles and some of their integral features
- list some of the specific house styles unique to each common style and some of their characteristic features
- recognize the elements that are typical of one style or another

3. Quick Quiz 3 is included at the end. The answers can be written in your book.

Key Words:

- *Ancient Classical*
- *Greek Revival*
- *Renaissance Classical*
- *Italianate*
- *French Colonial*
- *Georgian*
- *Adam*
- *Colonial Revival*
- *Medieval*
- *Gothic*
- *Victorian*
- *Tudor*
- *Queen Anne*
- *Stick*
- *Modern*
- *Arts and Crafts*
- *Machine age*
- *Prairie-style*
- *Craftsman*
- *Spanish Colonial*
- *Mission*

► 4.0 GENERAL ARCHITECTURAL CATEGORIES

In this section, we'll describe some of the common house styles and their defining features. We'll start by breaking houses into groups to simplify the discussion.

4.1 ANCIENT CLASSICAL

This is a style of architecture that is more common on government and institutional buildings than single family homes, but is directly influenced by the classical Greek and Roman buildings. The influence of Greek temples on these homes can be significant. Integral features include –

*   columns
*   symmetry
*   low roof slopes
*   bold entablatures

Subclasses include **early classic Revival**, **Greek Revival** and **Neoclassical**.

4.2 RENAISSANCE CLASSICAL

These are basically influenced by European interpretations of the original Greek and Roman classics. Subclasses include **Italianate**, **French Colonial** and **English** styles such as **Georgian**, **Adam** and **Colonial Revival**. In these houses, symmetry is again important. Details at windows, doors and eaves were often distinctive.

The Italian styles often included quoining, cornice brackets and arched windows. Dentils and pilasters are often integral components as well.

The French-style Renaissance homes often feature a steep roof, sometimes with sweeping lines. The roofs were often mansard and frequently incorporated dormers.

The English styles very often focused the eye on the front door with pediments, fanlights, transom lights and pilasters, for example.

4.3 MEDIEVAL

The next major styles are medieval. These are styles that largely come from France and England, and usually have a strong influence from churches and cathedrals. **Gothic**, **Victorian**, **Romanesque**, **Tudor** and **Queen Anne** are examples of medieval classes of architecture. Medieval architecture is usually asymmetric. Roofs are often a predominant feature of the building. Steep roofs are common. Chimneys are frequently featured in the architecture. There are some castle influences, and parapets, turrets and towers are common.

Gothic style architecture typically has the characteristic pointed arch windows associated with churches.

Gothic Revival typically has a steep gabled roof with an equally steep, full height cross gable at the center. In Gothic Revival, the windows typically extend up into the gables.

Queen Anne styles often feature porches that wrap around two sides of the house. These homes typically highlight chimneys and may include towers.

Tudor-style homes are very often a combination of masonry and stucco with the stucco set in half-timbering.

4.4 MODERN

Modern architecture is a twentieth century style. It tends to be simple and avoids copying details from older buildings. **Arts and Crafts** and **Machine Age** are two general classifications of modern buildings.

Arts and Crafts homes may be divided into **Prairie** style and **Craftsman** style homes. The Prairie style is often associated with Frank Lloyd Wright. The houses tended to have low-sloped roofs with wide overhangs. There was a strong emphasis on horizontal lines. False gable beams were popular.

The Craftsman style also had a low-sloped roof with wide overhangs. Exposed structural members on the exterior were common. Tapered pillars on porches are characteristic of Craftsman-style homes.

The more modern Machine Age buildings eliminated decoration almost entirely. Flat roofs with no overhang are common. Walls broken up into irregularly sized rectangles are common. In some cases, curved exterior walls are found. The most striking feature of these homes is the lack of exterior detailing.

4.5 SPANISH STYLE

The Spanish influence is strongest in the southern United States. Spanish influences can lead to either simple or detailed buildings. Classes include **Spanish Colonial**, **Mission**, **Pueblo Revival** and **Monterey**. Houses may be one- or two-story, although many examples are single-story. Exterior walls are typically adobe or stucco. Roofs are often red tiled. Repeated arches, exposed roof timbers and arched windows are common Spanish influences.

► 5.0 SPECIFIC HOUSE STYLES

Now we'll look briefly at some specific styles and their defining features.

5.1 ANCIENT CLASSICAL

We'll look first at two examples of the ancient classical style.

5.1.1 EARLY CLASSICAL REVIVAL

These homes were typically built in the late 1700s and early 1800s. They include large entry porches or porticos, usually supported by columns. The porch roof has a centered gable. Fanlights over the front door and sometimes in the gable are common. Windows line up both horizontally and vertically. These houses are symmetrical. They are most common in the southeastern United States.

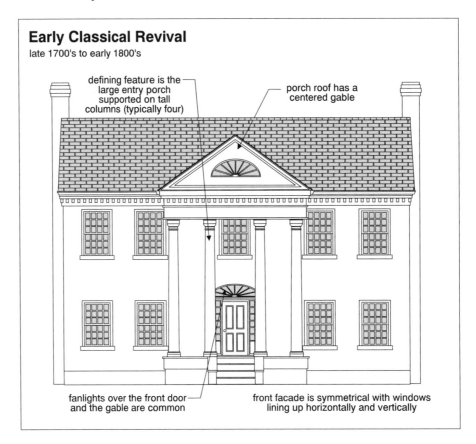

Early Classical Revival
late 1700's to early 1800's

defining feature is the large entry porch supported on tall columns (typically four)

porch roof has a centered gable

fanlights over the front door and the gable are common

front facade is symmetrical with windows lining up horizontally and vertically

5.1.2 GREEK REVIVAL

National

Greek Revival homes were common in the mid 1800's. They have a gabled or hipped roof that is usually low-sloped. Very bold cornice details forming an **entablature** with a **frieze** above an **architrave** are typical. Porches are common. The porch might be only over the front door or might extend the full width of the house. Columns are commonly used to support the porch roof. Transom and side lights around the front door are common. This is sometimes called the **National** style. These houses are common throughout the eastern United States and are found on the West Coast as well.

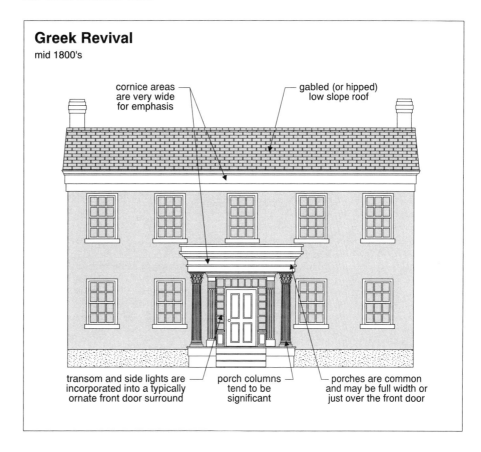

Greek Revival
mid 1800's

cornice areas are very wide for emphasis

gabled (or hipped) low slope roof

transom and side lights are incorporated into a typically ornate front door surround

porch columns tend to be significant

porches are common and may be full width or just over the front door

5.2 RENAISSANCE CLASSICAL

Now we'll look at five examples of the renaissance classical styles.

5.2.1 GEORGIAN

Georgian houses were popular through the 1700s. The front door is typically gabled with transom windows, decorative pilasters and a crown (entablature) over the front door. The cornice usually has decorative moldings such as dentils. Windows are typically double-hung with each sash having nine or twelve panes. Wood muntins (dividers between panes) are common. Windows are always separate (not grouped in pairs). The roof types can be side gabled, hipped or gambrel.

Georgian-style homes were very popular and a predominant style in the eastern United States.

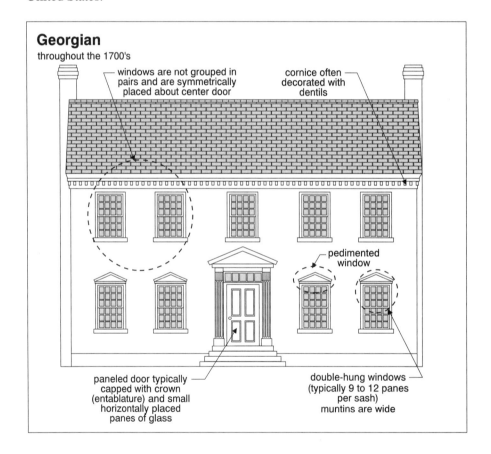

5.2.2 THE ADAM

The Adam is a variation on a Georgian style. It is also referred to as **Federal** style. It was common in the late 1700s and early 1800s. The Adam style is often three stories. Like the Georgian style, the Adam homes are symmetrical and the cornice work often includes dentils. Windows are typically double-hung and there are usually six panes of glass per window. Windows were never arranged in pairs, although Palladian windows are fairly common. The front door typically has a fanlight, often with sidelights and elaborate pilasters and crown.

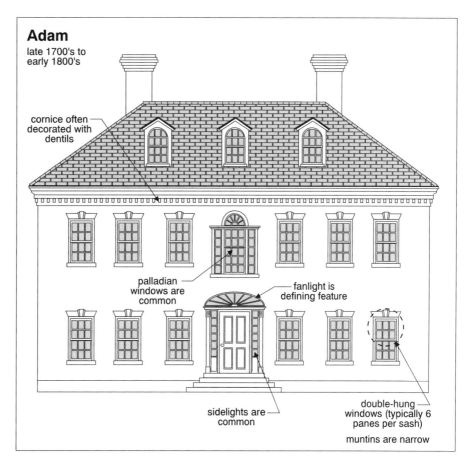

Narrow Muntins

This style of home was very popular through the entire eastern half of the United States. One of the distinguishing details between Georgian and Adam style houses is the muntins in the windows. Adam-style windows have a very narrow muntin, usually between ½ and ¾ inch wide. The muntins on Georgian windows are typically 1¼ inch wide.

5.2.3 COLONIAL REVIVAL

Colonial Revival houses were popular in the late 1800s and up until the mid 1900s. The focal point of the house is usually the front door, which includes a decorative crown and pilasters. Fanlights and sidelights are common. The front door is often protected by an entry porch or portico, typically with delicate columns. The houses are roughly symmetrical, although windows can be of varying sizes. A pair of windows on the main floor, for example, may not be repeated on the second floor. Windows are typically double-hung with multi-glazing in at least one of the sashes. Again, these were common throughout North America.

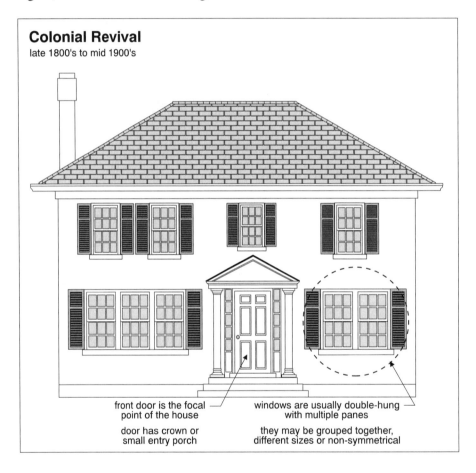

Colonial Revival
late 1800's to mid 1900's

front door is the focal point of the house

door has crown or small entry porch

windows are usually double-hung with multiple panes

they may be grouped together, different sizes or non-symmetrical

5.2.4 ITALIAN RENAISSANCE

Arches And
Brackets

Italian Renaissance houses were common in the very late 1800s and early 1900s. They typically have a low-pitched hipped roof covered with clay tiles. The second story windows are typically smaller than the first floor windows. Arches above doors and on first story windows are common. There are usually small columns or pilasters on the front entrance and the facade is typically symmetrical. The roof typically has a large overhang with decorative brackets supporting the eaves. Recessed front porches are common, some with multiple arches.

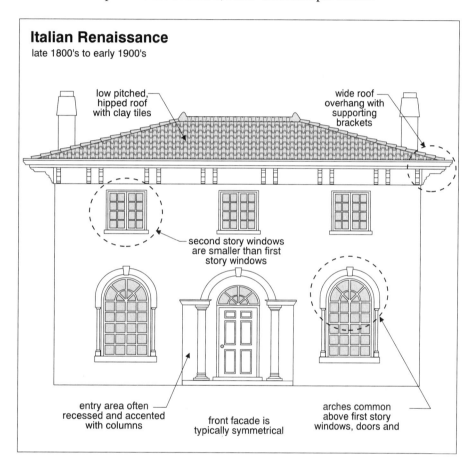

Italian Renaissance
late 1800's to early 1900's

low pitched, hipped roof with clay tiles

wide roof overhang with supporting brackets

second story windows are smaller than first story windows

entry area often recessed and accented with columns

front facade is typically symmetrical

arches common above first story windows, doors and

43

5.2.5 ITALIANATE

Cupolas And
Quoining

Italianate houses were popular through the middle part of the 1800s. They were typically two- or three-story houses. The roofs are usually low-sloped and often hipped. The roof overhangs are wide and decorative brackets below are common. Windows are typically tall and narrow with rounded or curved tops. Windows can be arranged in pairs.

A cupola or tower in the center of the roof is sometimes present. Quoined details and belt courses are common on some Italianate homes. Porch columns are often slender and columns are often used in groups of two or three.

Italianate houses are common in the Midwest and out to the West Coast. On the East Coast, they are more common in the northern than the southern half of the eastern seaboard.

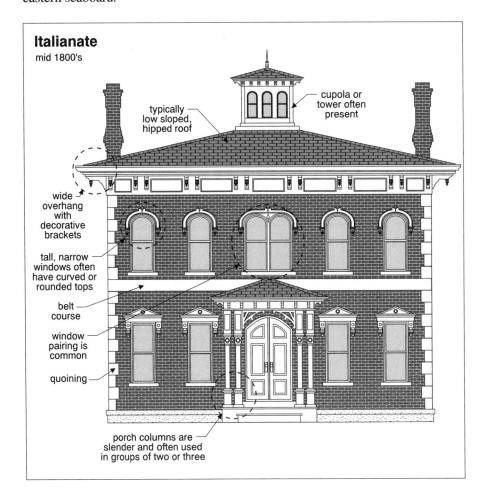

Italianate
mid 1800's

cupola or tower often present

typically low sloped, hipped roof

wide overhang with decorative brackets

tall, narrow windows often have curved or rounded tops

belt course

window pairing is common

quoining

porch columns are slender and often used in groups of two or three

5.3 MEDIEVAL

Now, we'll look at some of the medieval styles.

5.3.1 GOTHIC REVIVAL

This is a less common style than many we've discussed.

Steep Roofs And Gables — Gothic Revival homes were typically built in the mid to late 1800s. Gothic Revival homes have a steeply pitched roof, usually with steep cross gables. The gables often have decorative trim (vergeboards). Gothic Revival homes are most often light browns and pinks. The wall surface from the main floor usually extends up into the gable.

Arched Windows — Windows often extend up into the gables as well. A pointed arch window is typical and front porches are usually present and often full width. Windows can be bay or oriel. Glazing within sashes is sometimes in a diamond pattern. A drip mold over windows is common.

Finial — Gable trim may include a **finial** (decorative elements at the top of a gable, spire or other peak) or cross bracing.

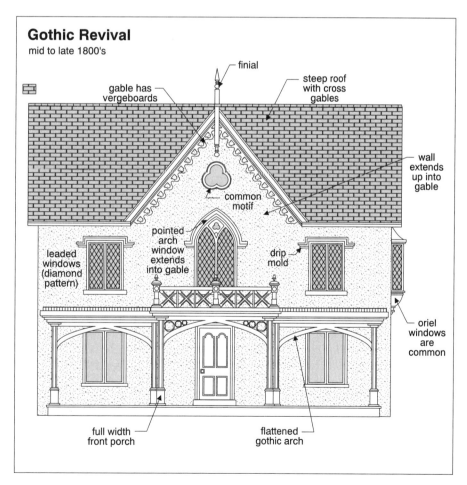

Gothic Revival
mid to late 1800's

- finial
- gable has vergeboards
- steep roof with cross gables
- common motif
- wall extends up into gable
- pointed arch window extends into gable
- leaded windows (diamond pattern)
- drip mold
- oriel windows are common
- full width front porch
- flattened gothic arch

5.3.2 STICK

Gables And Trusses

Stick houses were built in the latter half of the 1800s. They typically included a steep gable roof, usually with cross gables. Decorative trusses are often located near the top of the gable. Exposed rafter ends at the eaves are common.

Colors

Stick style homes are typically painted with the siding one color and the raised trim in a contrasting color. Stick (Eastlake) houses are often painted in bold, contrasting color schemes with lots of rich and bright colors including reds, greens, yellows and blues. Walls are typically shingles or horizontal boards, often interrupted with vertical, horizontal or diagonal boards laid over the siding surface to emphasize the look.

Porches often have curved or diagonal braces. The multi-textured wall surfaces and trusses at the gables define this style.

These are most common in the northeastern United States, although it is not a predominant style. The Stick style can be thought of as a link between the Gothic Revival and Queen Anne styles.

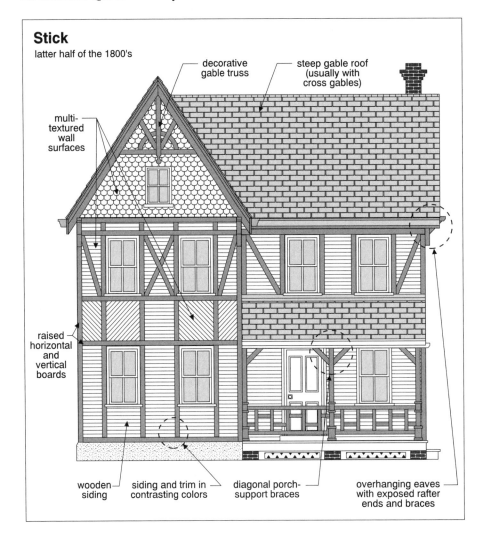

Stick
latter half of the 1800's

- decorative gable truss
- steep gable roof (usually with cross gables)
- multi-textured wall surfaces
- raised horizontal and vertical boards
- wooden siding
- siding and trim in contrasting colors
- diagonal porch-support braces
- overhanging eaves with exposed rafter ends and braces

5.3.3 QUEEN ANNE

Gingerbread

Queen Anne-style houses were common in the late 1800s and early 1900s. Queen Anne style homes were very common in many areas of North America during the relatively short period in which they were built. They typically have complex, steeply pitched roofs with a large front-facing gable. Gable ornamentation is sometimes referred to as **gingerbread** or **Eastlake** (named after the English furniture designer).

Patterned Shingles

Patterned wood or clay shingles are common. Shingles were often textured or detailed to provide a focal point. Some Queen Anne homes are half-timbered in the Tudor style and a few have patterned masonry. Queen Anne homes typically have very few flat wall surfaces.

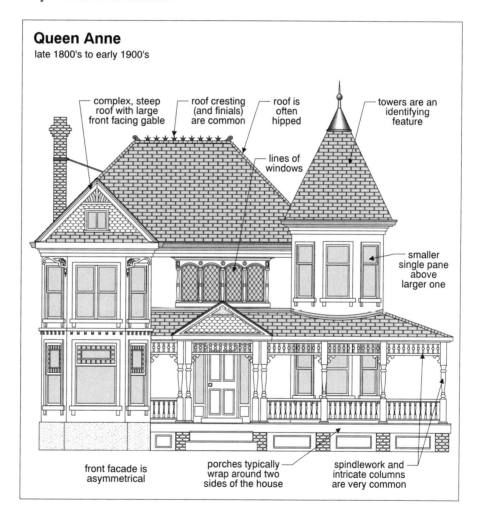

Queen Anne
late 1800's to early 1900's

complex, steep roof with large front facing gable

roof cresting (and finials) are common

roof is often hipped

towers are an identifying feature

lines of windows

smaller single pane above larger one

front facade is asymmetrical

porches typically wrap around two sides of the house

spindlework and intricate columns are very common

Wrap-around Porches

Queen Anne style homes are typically painted in rich and contrasting colors with lots of variety. Bay windows are common and front porches with decorative columns typically wrap around two sides of the house.

A tower at one corner of the front facade is common in Queen Anne style. Houses are typically asymmetrical. Chimneys are often patterned and large.

Turned spindles and decorative friezes on porches are common. Roof cresting and finials are also popular.

Grouped Casement Windows

Door and window surrounds are typically simple, perhaps because the walls are so busy. Window sashes may be single pane, although smaller panes above larger panes are common. Grouping of windows is also common in Queen Anne style. Queen Anne homes often had banks of windows. Casement windows are common and the upper panes frequently include stained glass.

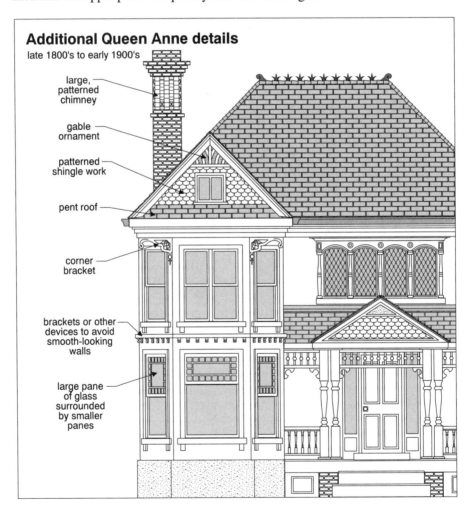

Additional Queen Anne details
late 1800's to early 1900's

large, patterned chimney

gable ornament

patterned shingle work

pent roof

corner bracket

brackets or other devices to avoid smooth-looking walls

large pane of glass surrounded by smaller panes

5.3.4 SHINGLE

Shingle-style homes were mostly built in the late 1800s. The wall and roof systems are typically wood shingle, although the shingling may be only on the second story. The wood roofing is now typically replaced with asphalt shingles. The walls at outside corners are typically unbroken by corner boards. The facades are irregular and rooflines were steep.

Eyebrow Dormers

Hip and eyebrow dormers are much more common than gable dormers. Intersecting cross gables and multiple level eaves are typical of Shingle-style homes and relate them to the Queen Anne style. Porches are usually extensive and may wrap around two sides of the home.

While the Queen Anne style focused on avoiding flat wall surfaces, the Shingle-style has lots of flat wall surfaces drawing one's eye to the shape of the building, rather than the wall texture. Towers and half towers are found on some Shingle-style homes. Porch railings and columns tend to be simple. Windows are very often multi-pane on the upper sash and single pane on the lower sash. Shingle-style homes frequently have a very small roof overhang at gable ends.

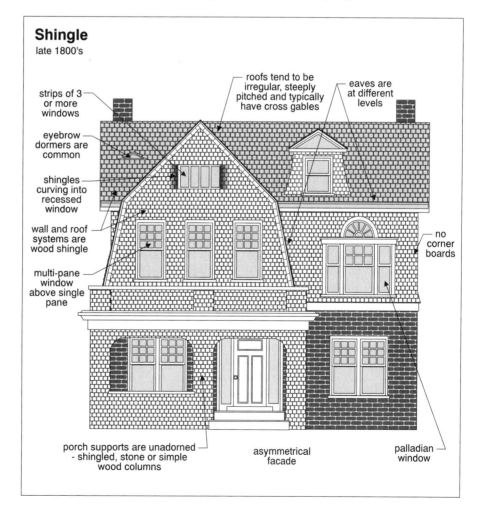

Shingle
late 1800's

strips of 3 or more windows

roofs tend to be irregular, steeply pitched and typically have cross gables

eaves are at different levels

eyebrow dormers are common

shingles curving into recessed window

wall and roof systems are wood shingle

multi-pane window above single pane

no corner boards

porch supports are unadorned - shingled, stone or simple wood columns

asymmetrical facade

palladian window

5.3.5 TUDOR

Half-timbering Tudor-style homes were most popular in the first 40 years of the twentieth century. These homes often have a lot of emphasis on roofs and chimneys. Tudor homes have steep pitched roofs and are usually side-gabled with one or more cross gables at the front, also steeply pitched. Decorative half-timbering is very common. Tall, narrow windows, sometimes with leaded muntins are common. Windows are usually grouped. Chimneys are usually massive and their pots at the top are decorative.

Gable details can include decorative vergeboards. The half-timbering infill is usually stucco, although it can be brick. Double-hung and casement windows are popular. Entrance doors often have rounded tops. Oriel windows are also common.

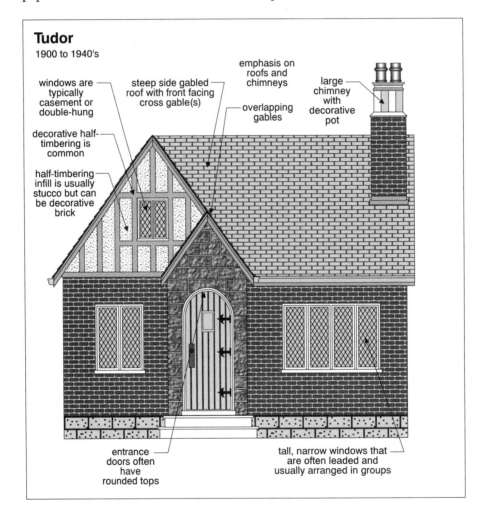

Tudor
1900 to 1940's

windows are typically casement or double-hung

steep side gabled roof with front facing cross gable(s)

emphasis on roofs and chimneys

large chimney with decorative pot

overlapping gables

decorative half-timbering is common

half-timbering infill is usually stucco but can be decorative brick

entrance doors often have rounded tops

tall, narrow windows that are often leaded and usually arranged in groups

5.4 MODERN

Now, let's have a look at some modern-style homes.

5.4.1 PRAIRIE

Prairie-style houses were common in the first 20 years of the twentieth century. They have very low pitched roofs that are usually hipped. The roofs have a wide overhang. Houses are typically two stories and there is often a one-story porch projecting out in front, or a one-story wing to the house. Porch supports are usually square, masonry and usually massive.

Horizontal Lines Stressed

Wall detailing emphasizing horizontal lines is common. Walls are typically light colored brick, stucco or wood. Windows are typically casements arranged in hori zontal groups. Stained glass, and geometric window glazing patterns are also widely found. These houses originated in the Chicago suburbs. Glazing patterns that include a large central pane with smaller perimeter panes are typical of some Prairie-style homes.

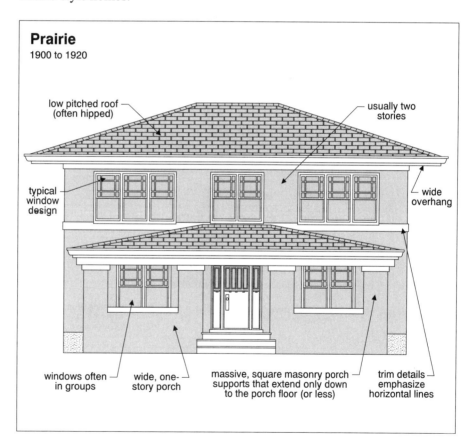

Prairie
1900 to 1920

low pitched roof
(often hipped)

usually two
stories

typical window design

wide overhang

windows often in groups

wide, one-story porch

massive, square masonry porch supports that extend only down to the porch floor (or less)

trim details emphasize horizontal lines

5.4.2 CRAFTSMAN

Exposed Rafters

Craftsman homes were also popular in the first 30 years of the twentieth century. They have low pitched gable roofs, often with the gable at the front of the house. The roof overhangs are generous and decorative beams or braces under the gables are common. Rafters are usually exposed at the eaves.

Craftsman-style homes are typically unpainted. Wood is left to weather naturally. Stucco is also left unpainted. Front porches are usually an extension of the roofline and can be full or part width. Columns supporting porch roofs are often tapered squares. Dormers are typically gabled.

Bungalow

This style originated in California and is most common there. These houses are often one story and have been called **bungalow** style.

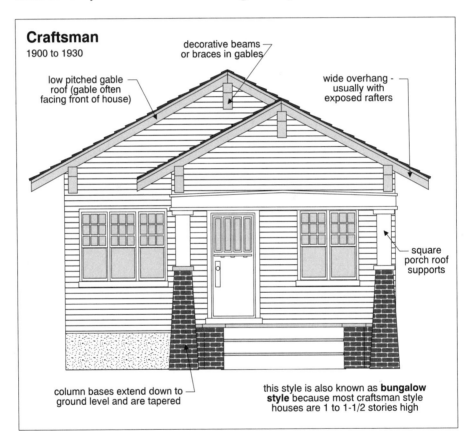

Craftsman
1900 to 1930

decorative beams or braces in gables

low pitched gable roof (gable often facing front of house)

wide overhang - usually with exposed rafters

square porch roof supports

column bases extend down to ground level and are tapered

this style is also known as **bungalow style** because most craftsman style houses are 1 to 1-1/2 stories high

5.4.3 MODERNISTIC

Modernistic homes were built typically from the 1920s to the 1940s, although, in some areas, these houses are still being built. Smooth wall surfaces that are usually stucco and flat roofs typify these buildings. If there is any detailing on the exterior facade, it is very often a horizontal line. The facades are usually asymmetric. One or more of the building faces or corners can be curved. Glass block is a common window treatment.

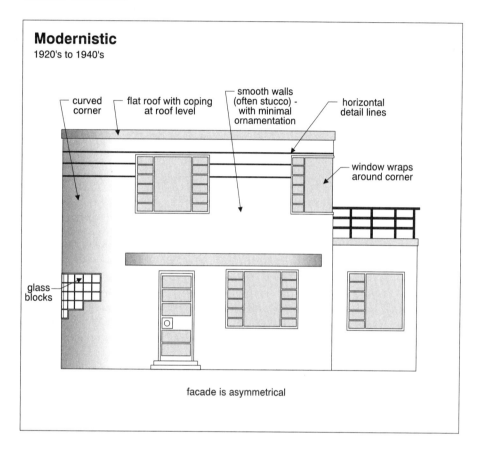

5.4.4 INTERNATIONAL

International homes were built from the 1920s until the present day. They are similar to Modernistic in that they have a flat roof, usually with no ledge or coping and asymmetric but very plain wall surfaces. Windows are usually metal casements set flush with the outer walls and there is very little ornamentation. Windows can be very large, in some cases floor to ceiling, in some cases wrapping around inside and outside corners. Cantilevered projections for balconies are common. These houses are relatively rare. Many have a decidedly institutional look.

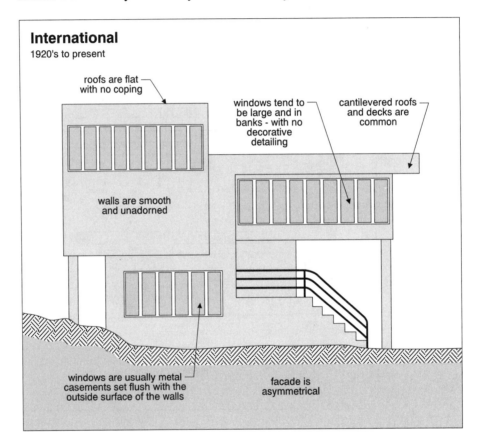

International
1920's to present

roofs are flat with no coping

windows tend to be large and in banks - with no decorative detailing

cantilevered roofs and decks are common

walls are smooth and unadorned

windows are usually metal casements set flush with the outside surface of the walls

facade is asymmetrical

5.5 SPANISH

5.5.1 SPANISH COLONIAL

Spanish Colonial architecture in North America dates back to 1600. They are typically one story with low-pitched or flat roofs. Flat roof examples typically have parapets. The walls are usually very thick and are made of adobe brick or stone covered with stucco.

There is often more than one exterior door. Doorways are very simple. Windows are very small and often had interior wooden shutters.

This type of architecture is most common in the southwestern United States. These buildings rarely had porches on the front facade.

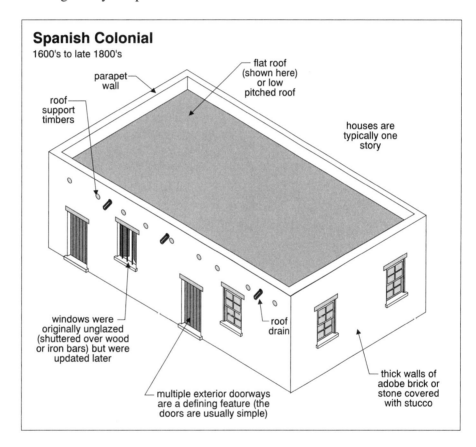

Spanish Colonial
1600's to late 1800's

parapet wall

roof support timbers

flat roof (shown here) or low pitched roof

houses are typically one story

windows were originally unglazed (shuttered over wood or iron bars) but were updated later

roof drain

multiple exterior doorways are a defining feature (the doors are usually simple)

thick walls of adobe brick or stone covered with stucco

5.5.2 MISSION

Mission-style homes were built originally in California in the late 1800s and early 1900s. They are characterized by the Mission dormer or roof parapet. Roof coverings are typically red clay tile. Roof overhangs are usually generous and rafter ends are exposed. Piers supporting front porches are usually large and square. Wall surfaces are usually smooth stucco. These homes may be symmetric or asymmetric.

Arched Openings On Porches

Some have a bell tower. **Quatrefoil** windows are common to the Mission style, as are multiple arched openings on porches.

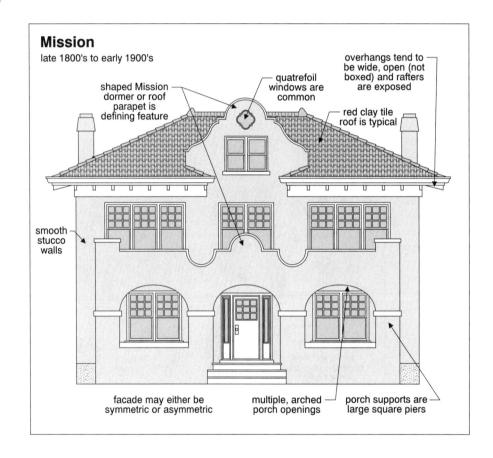

Mission
late 1800's to early 1900's

shaped Mission dormer or roof parapet is defining feature

quatrefoil windows are common

overhangs tend to be wide, open (not boxed) and rafters are exposed

red clay tile roof is typical

smooth stucco walls

facade may either be symmetric or asymmetric

multiple, arched porch openings

porch supports are large square piers

5.6 MISCELLANEOUS

Two well known styles of homes that are common in New England deserve discussion here.

5.6.1 CAPE COD

The Cape Cod home is a one-and-a-half-story home that is usually one-and-a-half rooms deep. There are typically no dormers and there is a central front door. These houses were first built in the 1700s and this style has been carried on and modified into the twentieth century. The walls of a Cape Cod house are typically white clapboard or shingle.

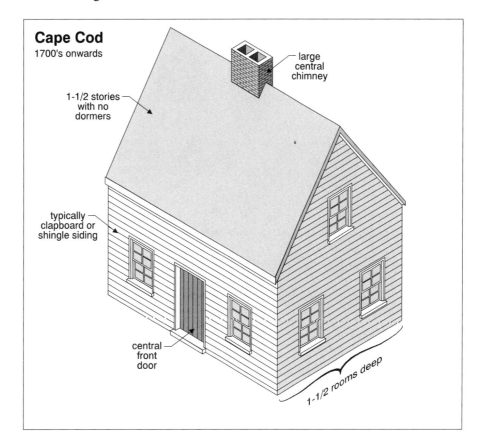

Cape Cod
1700's onwards

large central chimney

1-1/2 stories with no dormers

typically clapboard or shingle siding

central front door

1-1/2 rooms deep

5.6.2 SALTBOX

Saltbox houses were built in the first half of the 1700s. This is a two-story home that is one-and-a-half rooms deep. The defining feature is a simple gable roof with the rear slope longer than the front slope. The pitch of the front and rear slopes is sometimes the same, although these could vary. In some cases, the front slope is a lower pitch. A single central chimney typifies a saltbox house.

Early saltbox houses were unpainted. The wood weathered to a barnboard brown-gray. Reproduction saltbox houses are typically stained. If painted, they are typically white, brown or red.

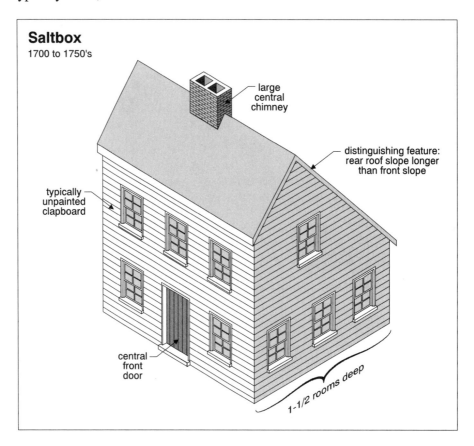

Saltbox
1700 to 1750's

- large central chimney
- distinguishing feature: rear roof slope longer than front slope
- typically unpainted clapboard
- central front door
- 1-1/2 rooms deep

Summary

While it's not necessary to identify house styles definitively, and it's probably risky to try to classify houses, you should be able to recognize the elements that are typical of one style or another. In your area, some styles will dominate. There may be some styles that you never see. Your credibility as a building expert will be enhanced by your knowledge of local architecture. Your inspection abilities will also be enhanced as you come to understand the vulnerable spots of various architectural details.

Architectural Styles
M O D U L E

QUICK QUIZ 3

☑ INSTRUCTIONS

• Write your answers in the spaces provided.

• Check your answers against ours at the back of the book after the Final Exercise.

• If you have trouble with the Quiz, reread the Study Session and try the Quiz again.

1. Ancient classical styles include _____ and _____ buildings.

2. Name four integral features and three of the subclasses of ancient classical buildings.

   _____

   _____

   _____

   _____

3. Porches are common on ancient classical houses.
   True ☐   False ☐

4. Georgian, Italianate, French Colonial, and Adam are subclasses of what common style?

   _____

5. Medieval architecture is usually asymmetric.
   True ☐   False ☐

6. Name five specific examples of medieval architecture.

_____

_____

_____

_____

_____

7. What feature is most often predominant in medieval-style houses?

_____

8. Arts and Crafts and Machine Age are two general classifications of what type of architecture?

_____

9. What is the most striking feature of Machine Age buildings?

_____

10. Flat roofs are common to both Modernistic and International homes.
True ☐   False ☐

11. Name four subclasses of Spanish-style architecture.

_____

_____

_____

_____

12. Are steep roofs more common in medieval styles or modern styles?

_____

13. What is usually the focal point of Colonial Revival houses?

_____

14. When were Italian Renaissance houses common?

_____

15. List four elements common to Italianate houses.

_____

_____

_____

_____

16. Stick houses are often painted in bold colors.
True ☐   False ☐

17. Stick style can be thought of as a link between _____
and _____ styles.

18. When were Queen Anne houses commonly built?

_____

19. Queen Anne houses often have towers.
True ☐   False ☐

20. Gable ornamentation on Queen Anne houses is called _____
or _____

21. What can be said of Queen Anne house wall surfaces?

_____

22. What kind of dormers are common on Shingle-style houses?

_____

23. When were Tudor-style homes popular?

_____

24. The most common design element of Tudor-style homes is

_____

25. Tudor-style homes usually have hip roofs.
True ☐   False ☐

26. Describe porch supports for Prairie-style homes.

_____

_____

27. On Craftsman-style houses, are roof overhangs large or small?

_____

28. Vivid painting is a characteristic of Craftsman-style houses.
True ☐   False ☐

29. List three features of Modernistic houses.

_____

_____

_____

30. _____ windows are common to the Mission style.

31. How can one distinguish between a Cap Cod and a Saltbox home?

_____

Key Words:
- *Ancient Classical*
- *Greek Revival*
- *Renaissance Classical*
- *Italianate*
- *French Colonial*
- *Georgian*
- *Adam*
- *Colonial Revival*
- *Medieval*
- *Gothic*
- *Victorian*
- *Tudor*
- *Queen Anne*
- *Stick*
- *Modern*
- *Arts and Crafts*
- *Machine Age*
- *Prairie-Style*
- *Craftsman*
- *Spanish Colonial*
- *Mission*

► ANSWERS TO QUICK QUIZZES

Answers to Quick Quiz 1

1. Rectangular

2. • Detached
  • Semi detached
  • Townhouse or rowhouse

3. Urban

4. A linear plan house is 1 room deep. A massed plan house is 2 or more rooms deep.

5. They don't shed snow.

6. Gambrel or Dutch Colonial

7. • Shed
  • Gable
  • Butterfly
  • Hip
  • Gambrel
  • Mansard

8. Dutch Colonial

9. Flat roofs focus on walls, pitched roofs on roofs.

10. • Pinnacle
  • Cupola
  • Turret

11. Decorative iron railings and a flat roof

12. Decorative wood trim on gables

13. • Keeps walls dry
  • Shields windows from sunlight
  • Strong impact on architectural style

14. They form architectural focal points.

15. • Gable
  • Hip
  • Arched
  • Shed
  • Inset
  • Flat
  • Eyebrow
  • Segmental

Quick Quiz 2

1. Cornice or entablature

2. A small row of blocks, like teeth, found on the cornice.

3. Wall corners that have rectangular blocks of a different color and/or texture than the rest of the wall.

4. Tudor style homes have half timbering and nogging, and are often stucco.

5. • Single hung
   • Double hung
   • Casement
   • Slider
   • Fixed
   • Awning
   • Hopper
   • Louver (jalousie)

6. A sliding window with no metal, vinyl or wood frame around the moveable glass portion.

7. A hopper tilts in, pivoting at the bottom. An awning swings out, pivoting at the top.

8. Warm climates

9. Muntins are decorative only; they help define the architectural style of the house.

10. See illustration in section 3.7

11. At the top of a window.

12. Oriel windows do not extend to the ground.

13. False

14. A pilaster is a projection from the wall, rather than an independent column.

15. • Doric
   • Tuscan
   • Ionic
   • Corinthian

Quick Quiz 3

1. Government and institutional buildings

2. Integral Features
- Columns
- Symmetry
- Low slope roofs
- Bold entablatures

Subclasses
- Early Classic Revival
- Greek Revival
- Neoclassical

3. False

4. Renaissance Classical

5. True

6. • Gothic
   - Victorian
   - Romanesque
   - Tudor
   - Queen Anne

7. Roofs

8. Modern

9. Lack of exterior detailing.

10. True

11. • Spanish Colonial
   - Mission
   - Pueblo Revival
   - Monterey

12. Medieval

13. The front door

14. Late 1800s to early 1900s

15. • Low sloped hip roofs
   - Wide roof overhang with decorative brackets
   - Tall narrow windows with rounded tops
   - Slender columns in groups, on porches

16. True

17. Gothic revival and Queen Anne styles

18. Late 1800s to early 1900s

19. True

20. Gingerbread, or Eastlake

21. Very few flat wall surfaces.

22. Hip and eyebrow dormers

23. 1900 to 1940s

24. Roofs and chimneys

25. False

26. Massive, square masonry porch supports.

27. Large

28. False

29. • Smooth walls
   • Flat roofs with coping
   • Facade is asymmetrical

30 Quatrefoil

31. A saltbox is 2-story in front, 1-story in back. The back roof is longer than the front. A Cape Cod has a symmetric roof.